Arrogant Bones

Guillaume —

Arrogance is no sin

in verse

Gary Geddes

Also by Larry Schug

Scales Out of Balance: Poems by Lawrence Schug, 1990.

Caution Thin Ice: Poems by Lawrence Schug, 1993.

The Turning of Wheels: Poems by Larry Schug, 2001.

Arrogant Bones

Poems

by

Larry Schug

NORTH STAR PRESS OF ST. CLOUD, INC.

St. Cloud, Minnesota

Dedication

To Juli
An Earth Keeper

Cover photo: Larry Schug
Author photo: Stuart Goldschen

This book is printed on 100%
post-consumer recycled content.

Printed in the United States of America

Published by
North Star Press of St. Cloud, Inc.
P.O. Box 451
St. Cloud, Minnesota 56302

northstarpress.com
info@northstarpress.com

Acknowledgements

The following poems were originally published in the following magazines, anthologies or e-zines. Thank you to all the editors and patrons and readers of these publications.

"The Way Horses Are," "Kirby Puckett," "Come Home," "The Honor Guard at George Mueller's Funeral," "Neighborhood Mothers," "A Minor Death in Indigo," "Barn," "Coal Train," "You Give Me an African Sunset," "Counting Hummingbirds in a Time of War," "Lucy's House," "On the Other Side of His Tears" and "Don't Listen to Leonard Cohen" in *Main Channel Voices*.

"Old Crow" and "Territory" in *Fire Ring Voices*.

"Construction Accident" in *re:Verse*.

"Birches" in *Connections*.

"Eleven Whitetail Deer" and "Waterfall" in *North Coast Review*.

"Peat Fire" in *Wired Hearts*.

"Arrogant Bones" and "Preparing the Fields" in *Prairie Poetry*.

"Darjeeling" and "Border Crossing" in *California Quarterly*.

"Mars," "On That Rainy Sunday," "The Old Haunts," "Elephant Bell #2," "Dirty Hands" and "Barber and Son" in *The Talking Stick*.

Table of Contents

I. Grateful for the Dead

II. In a Time of War

III. A Place of Healing, of Miracles

IV. Inside a Greater Light

V. Arrogant Bones

VI. Between Mars and Mexico

VII. I Should've Taken Creative Writing

I. *Grateful for the Dead*

The Way Horses Are
(for Roger W. Young)

He was silent for a moment,
then came back on the line,
a catch in his voice.
He said his horse,
standing at the corral fence,
had been looking toward the house
since early this morning.
He's looking for me, he said,
doesn't understand
I don't have the strength any more
to go out and feed him, brush him,
scratch his ears.
He choked up again, said
that horse would wait for him
'til the end of its days,
unaware he'd reached the end of his.
That's just the way horses are.
My friend can't see me,
but I'm standing beside that horse
and I'll be looking for him
until the end of my days, too,
wishing we could talk once more.
That's just the way friends are.

On That Rainy Sunday

I didn't know,
though you might have,
that you'd be gone by Monday;
a good soul
driving a broken-down truck
on a ten mile downhill run
with nine miles worth of brakes.
You couldn't get out of bed,
your body ravished by that god damn cancer,
yet when I entered your room
a light sparked to life in your eyes,
you hugged me with bony arms
like all your wood-cutter's strength
had returned, summoned by sheer willpower.
As I pressed my face into your neck,
you must've felt my tears, warm on your skin;
tears of joy as much as of grief,
both of us knowing that all the years
had come down to this one moment
and that this moment would have to last
forever.

One Sunday on La Prairie River

Casting a Lazy Ike, kinda lazy-like,
half asleep in sun and breeze,
when an owl's call,
strange for that time of day,
woke me from my day dream
to see a wreath of roses floating by,
followed by a single yellow rose,
then another, a pink blossom,
a red, a white, another yellow,
followed by fifty more roses,
turning slowly in the current.

I waded into the river,
plucked the roses from the stream,
as many as I could hold,
placed them in my cooler,
un-snagged the wreath from a deadfall,
found a ribbon that read,
"Husband and Father 1947–2006,
We'll Always Love You."
I set the wreath free, but kept the roses,
brought them home to my own wife and daughter,
thinking of that strange day-owl's call,
knowing, somehow that "Husband and Father"
wouldn't have minded at all.

Construction Accident

He'd been workin'
demolition sites
since Jericho;
thought he knew
all about
tumblin' walls.
But you know
them demo sites,
so noisy sometimes
you can't hear
a trumpet blow.

Welder

His obituary said he died suddenly;
his head, most likely, full of plans,
his welding shop full of unfinished jobs—
a tip-down antenna mast
he was building for a friend's brother,
the broken teeth he was fixing
on his neighbor's hay rake,
supposed to be done before the next cutting.

There was wire in the wire-feed welder,
the oxy-acetylene tanks were still half-full;
a good supply of rods and flux on hand.
His heavy leather gloves lay on the bench,
his face shield hanging on the wall,
a piece of iron clamped tight in a vice,
unswept slag on the cement floor.

I can't help but think of unfinished poems,
notebooks left open, scribbled words,
pens, like jumbled pick-up sticks
lying all over the desk;
all the things needing to be fixed
with a solid weld of words
for myself, my neighbors,
all the things that will stay broken forever.

Barber and Son

I

Sitting on a throne of scrolled brass,
worn leather, shiny porcelain,
I feel like a king as my father cuts my hair,
but am nonetheless told to sit still,
tilt my head this way, then that.
We don't say much.
We talk a little baseball, a little work,
but that's enough
for a prodigal father, a prodigal son,
who have returned to themselves
and to each other
after squandering so many years splitting hairs,
shaving close enough to draw blood,
finally realizing that when one of us bleeds,
so does the other.

II

Here he is at age thirty,
my first-born little boy,
coming to me for a haircut again;
surprising, after all the years
he avoided my clippers and scissors,
hair hanging to his shoulders.
Now he says he wouldn't know
where else to go.
The old-time barbershops are gone,
like the old-time barbers—
replaced by stylists, some of them, women
wielding blow combs, playing disco.
You'd never hear a ball game in these salons
and the magazines are all replaced
with each new issue—
Career Times and *Computer Weekly*
instead of a ragged *Field and Stream*,
certainly no *Soldier of Fortune* or *Boy's Life*.

I sweep my grown son's hair from the floor,
almost feel like keeping it; I don't know why.
I'm just glad he still comes by.

Kirby Puckett

Kirby Puckett is running around the bases in this poem
pumping his fist in the air
like he just sent the World Series into game seven,
though this is not a poem about Kirby Puckett.
This poem's about a story we've been told,
a story about death and a place we call Heaven.
This is a poem about my father and my brother—
both dead, as is Kirby Puckett;
this is a poem about me and you, alive.
We are alive, here and now,
and today, I choose to believe that heaven story
in order to picture Mike and my dad
and all the other dead Twins fans
waiting at the Pearly Gates, waving homer hankies
and giving Kirby Puckett high fives
as he crosses that final home plate,
hoping someone will be waiting somewhere for me.

Threads

She saves her hair in a grocery sack—
silken, silver strands,
that once hung to her waist,
coming out now in clumps
with each combing.
She's saving every thread until spring;
she'll scatter it in her yard
for jenny wrens and fat robins
to weave the fibers into nests,
for squirrels and little brown field mice
to pad the beds of spring litters.

Her daughter crochets cotton and wool
into caps of bright colors
to cover her mother's cold baldness;
but more than that, she weaves a thread
that binds them to each other,
weaves them both deeper
into the fabric of the world,
of life,
love.

Where All Roads End

In a black and white photo in the family album
my brother and I stand proudly beside brand new bicycles
beneath the Christmas tree.
As boys we rode them everywhere together through our town,
but in our teens, he bought a little black Corvair,
and I inherited the old man's '56 Pontiac.
We drove away from each other in our twenties and thirties.
He married young, left town with his bride,
followed a straight highway of religion and business,
his route precisely marked on a map, destination firmly in mind;
while I could never stay on any smooth highway,
choosing instead to wander metaphysical side roads and rutted trails.

We were both stubborn as stone those many years,
he, never veering from his route,
I, adamantly rambling just for the sake of roaming.
And now we've reached our forties, both mellowed with time,
but the doctors say he won't see fifty, his car has run out of gas,
while I still plod along, changing lanes and driving in circles.
I'm thankful that in these last miles we've decided to travel together,
having discovered that our destinations are really the same
and I hope he'll be waiting for me where all roads end.

A Day at the Beach

Between tears I watch you sleep;
so still, I wonder if the cancer
hasn't already taken you.
The storm has exhausted itself
over your land of muscle and bone;
slips over a horizon only you see.
The sea flattens to glass,
your breath, a shallow breeze,
blows over an eroded shoreline.
My spirit is a beach at low tide,
my sands have shifted forever.
My breathing shallows with yours.
The wind that blows through me
has become more precious
as I try to breathe for both of us.

The Old Haunts
(for Dan Viehauser)

I tell you, old friend,
even though you're dead,
you're welcome to visit
whenever you wish,
in whatever form you choose,
and though I may greet you
with laughter or tears,
know they come from the same place.
My house of memory is crowded
with old friends passing through,
some we shared in life,
others, I know will welcome you
and me too, when my time comes
and we must pass from house to house,
heart to heart to be remembered
until everyone who loved us
has migrated to the next place,
together again and having no need
to visit the old haunts anymore.

One Less Voice
(remembering Dave Ray)

He's gone away
like a guitar chord
fades into the next song;
yet he lingers on the way a song
hangs in the smoky air
of a bar closed up for the night,
then stays in your head for years.
So blow your old mouth harp;
in his memory, strum your guitar.
There's more blues appearing
on the doorstep each morning,
piling up day by day;
but one less voice,
both gentle and gruff,
to sing them ol' blues away.

The Luthier's Passing
(for Thomas Humphrey)

He left behind guitars, unfinished,
racks of rosewood, cedar, spruce,
spools of strings,
boxes of tuning pegs,
guitars conceived
but not yet born.
Like poems yet to find pen and paper,
songs are searching an ethereal realm
for exquisite strings to dance upon;
much the same as souls
searching for bodies in which to be born.

The Sound of Two Hands Dancing
(for Thomas Humphrey)

Tears fall tonight
All around this world
On the strings of elegant guitars,
Haunting melodies, softly played,
The sound of two hands dancing,
As songs set sail into the ether,
Bound for the safe harbors
Of the human heart.

After He Died #1

Unplayed notes
crouch in shadow,
skeletons
of old songs
left for dead,
hide in the harmonica's
unlit rooms.
Those beautiful blues
hovering all around,
wait like bums
in a train yard
for a whistle
from across the trestle.

Trinity

The summer after my mother died
my father and my brother
were eating breakfast together
at Steve's cabin in the woods near Ely,
when suddenly, Dad pointed out the window.
Steve, Steve, a fuckin' bear!
He was so excited he spilled his coffee.
Steve laughed until he was bent over.
Everyone knew the old man swore,
but no one'd ever heard him say fuckin' before.

Don't tell me there was no poetry
in this unlikely trinity,
I'll tell you that God was there
in the name of a father, a son and a fuckin' bear.

II. *In a Time of War*

Counting Hummingbirds in a Time of War

The cry of a rabbit
carried off by a hunting owl
unsettles you, keeps you awake
in anticipation of another owl,
another scream.
To put your mind at ease,
you count hummingbirds
in your head,
seen today, hovering
above a bed of red bee balm.
For a blessed moment,
the humming in your ears
is only the thrumming of tiny wings.
You think of a man lying in bed
in another part of the world,
almost insane from blood,
listening for helicopters
thrumming in the distance.
You resume counting hummingbirds
to keep your sanity.

Lucy's House

is a typical older house
on a typical, tree-lined street
in Waconia, Minnesota,
a typical American town.
Inside this house,
Lucy's mom is cleaning closets;
there is stuff all over the floor—
a guitar, clothes, backpacks, winter boots—
all the stuff people put in closets.
In this typical house
there are three parrots squawking all at once,
a collie named Bertha wearing a pink bow
and a gray and white border collie named Ringo
who is relentlessly herding a cat named Howard.
Lucy's brother and his friend are cutting marshmallows
to put in homemade ice cream
and Lucy is making margaritas for me and her
to drink while sitting on her front steps.
As we drink them, I wonder what's going on
in the two typical houses next to Lucy's
and in all the other typical houses in America,
while the typical houses of typical people
in Beirut, Baghdad, Tel Aviv and Kabul
are being bombed to dust
on this typical summer day
on our all but typical, one of a kind,
only place we can live in this universe, little planet.

Come Home

My damn dog's run away again
and I get so mad—
doesn't he know who feeds him?
I holler and holler,
yell 'til I'm hoarse;
America! America!
Come on home.
I know he can hear me
but he just ignores me
until he finally comes home
ragged and bloody, limping,
his tail tucked between his legs.
He's good for awhile,
but off in the distance
I hear another dog barking
and now he's perked up his ears,
his nose is in the air,
he's growling again.

The Honor Guard at George Mueller's Funeral

A cynical or unkind person
might be tempted to laugh at the old men,
bellies hanging over their belts,
hunched-over soldiers
wearing rumpled uniforms,
carrying rifles that seem like toys;
but the sorrow and dignity is real
as they "Present arms!"
These old soldiers are heroes;
they won The Big One,
made the world safe for awhile.

A half-century after their war,
one of their comrades has fallen.
After a twenty-one gun salute fired over a corn field
and "Taps" played on a tinny boom box,
two men fold the flag from the casket
into a perfect triangle, stars up,
present it to the veteran's widow, salute her stiffly.
They shuffle-march back to the church,
each man thinking of his own wife,
her tears falling one day
on a perfectly folded American flag.

The Neighborhood Mothers

Our WW II mothers hated us playing war,
threatened us with our fathers' belts
when we filled snowballs with stones
or stuck twigs in them
so they looked like land mines.

Our mothers got so angry
when we slashed at each other
with swords made of pine lathe,
or sling shot bbs and pebbles
over the heads of the rope-jumping Perrier girls,
as we tried to put out the lights of the Pelkey brothers
and their allies from across the alley, the Olsons.

But Louella Pelkey and Betty Perrier and Ruth Olson
and Evelyn Schug, too, let their sons go to war.
They were deathly afraid for us,
but told us how proud of us they were;
how handsome and manly we looked
when we came home from basic training
in our dress green uniforms
and same shaved heads
we wore during summer when we were kids.
Our mothers acted like our M-16s were pea-shooters,
like our howitzers harmlessly exploded stolen tomatoes
on the door of old man Umerski's dodge.

I wish my mom would've got me by the collar,
jerked me into the house, made me stay in my room
for the whole year of 1968.
In 1972, she told me she didn't know why she let me go.
Probably for the same reasons I went, I thought,
though neither of us could give voice to those reasons then.
She said she wished she would've grabbed my ear,
gave it a twist, and pulled me all the way to Winnipeg.
For both our own good.

Sacrifice

I was too slow to beat out grounders to deep shortstop,
stretch singles into doubles or steal bases
but I should've tried to run all the way to Canada
when Uncle called me to pinch hit
for some of his rich friends in Vietnam.
When I looked into the bleachers from the on-deck circle,
I saw my parents and little brothers
cheering me on to do what they thought was right.
I knew that in a town like St. Cloud,
where everybody's business is everybody's business,
that a lot of men and their sons would never get a haircut
at the barbershop of a pussy draft-dodger's father,
even if the boy was following his conscience.
The workers at the Veteran's Hospital would stay away
and so would the World War II and the Korean War vets
who worked at the refrigerator plant
across the street from my old man's shop.
My old man's shop was just a one-chair shop
but it had to feed six hungry boys,
which it barely did
and only because my mother worked a full time job, too.
My conscience signaled me to sacrifice.
It was the only play.

Backache

Here I am, bitching about a backache.
It hurts like all hell;
hurts to bend, to straighten up,
to sit, to stand;
hurts when I work, when I walk,
hurts when I just lie around;
but I tell myself to stop my damn whining,
my warm house, soft bed, full stomach,
American whining.

There are men in Baghdad and Beirut,
men whose backs ache just like mine,
though my back ache doesn't have to deal
with falling bombs, machine gun fire,
children crying for food.
There are men with backaches
whose wives are gone in their heads,
whose houses are reduced to rubble and ash,
men with backaches
stumbling through crumbling cities
with no water, no heat, no light;
men with backaches.

Caucasian

I'm classified as Caucasian
by government agencies
though I have never been
to the Caucasus Mountains
or Asia, for that matter,
but judging by the tint of my skin,
the shape of my face, I can guess
that somewhere in pre-European mist,
a peasant woman was raped by a soldier
in the army of one of the great Khans,
swooping into her village on horseback,
burning it to the ground,
killing her husband, father, and brothers.
Perhaps that's why I dream of horses,
know that nothing I have,
not even the blood in my veins,
has not been stolen from someone.

On the Other Side of His Tears

I find myself
looking for the old cat
in all the familiar places—
the desk chair upstairs,
the corner of the couch,
curled beside the knitted pillow.
I find myself reaching for her bowl
when I feed the other cat,

like a widow
or the mother of a fallen soldier,
who, without thinking
sets a place at the table
for someone no longer here,
like a father, inadvertently
cooling two beers in the fridge
before the ballgame begins,
then drinking both by himself,
the TV a blur
on the other side of his tears.

III. *A Place of Healing, of Miracles*

What Wild Mojo?
(The Gathering Place at Ghost Ranch)

How has the accumulation of my days
brought me to this place, this day,
from the northern farmlands
to this place of arroyos and mesas,
yodeling coyotes?
What have I done
to be deserving of this room
where I sit, contemplative,
among paintings and carvings,
a cup of Earl Gray at hand
and a view of majestic Pedernal,
miles away, yet in this same room?
What wild mojo has brought me here,
where warmth and serenity
surround me like the friends
who share the speaking rocks,
the singing sky,
the swirling, twirling dress
worn by the dancing desert?

Tsiping Mesa

Above the village of Cañones
I visit the home of a people
remembered by stone steps set in a trail
along side Tsiping Mesa;
people remembered by the ruins of stone houses,
crumbled-in kivas,
painted pottery shards scattered about.

If the people who built these steps,
created and decorated these earthen vessels
and worshipped in these kivas were still here,
they would most likely kill me
for the audacity of my trespass.
What they do instead
is rejoice in this cold wind,
my hunger and thirst,
my preoccupation with time
that drives me back to the valley floor
so that their spirits may rest once again
in the silence of these stones,
having repelled yet another invader.

El Farolito

Dios,
it's hotter'n hell
in this part of heaven—
steaming rice and beans hot,
green chili hot,
sweating forehead hot
at these little tables
where locals and touristas
crowd together to eat;
while others wait outside
along the main road
that runs through the old part of El Rito
to enter through a gate of heaven
where no one is judged,
all are fed in turn.
You think you've attained a state divine,
but, no; una vez mas maravilla!
You're served sopaipillas
drenched in honey.

In Chimayo

In the crypt of the Santuario de Chimayo
there is a place of healing,
of miracles,
of crutches left to hang on adobe walls
among icons brought here long ago from Spain;
left by the lame who now walk upright
because of faith placed in Jesus
and the healing power of raw earth.

In Chimayo
a beautiful woman with AIDS speaks to us
at the school where we volunteer today;
her little boy, her own miracle,
healer of her spirit if not her body, clings to her skirts.
She tells us she's paying for choices made years ago
and for trusting that cheating bastard ex-husband
who infected her.
This woman says she can live with her choices;
she has no choice but to do so,
having tried both Jesus and the Earth to no avail.
She asks only that we choose wisely
in whatever we do,
for the sake of children, unborn,
who may, one day, cling to us.

High Plains Illusion

Between Eagle Nest and Raton,
wind and a bumpy New Mexico two-lane
buffet the van, push it over the center line,
then nearly off the road's shoulder.
Brown foothills and blue mesas
seem suspended in dust and distance,
making it hard to tell if you're moving at all.
The horizon never seems to get any closer
though you know you're traveling
toward where earth becomes sky;
you just can't tell how far you have to go.
When you look in the rear-view mirror
you can't see where this journey began
or what pushed you in this direction.
All you can do is to keep your foot on the gas,
your hands on the wheel,
stay on the road the best you can.

Weavers

They come to Ghost Ranch,
the high desert of Georgia O'Keefe,
seeking patterns and colors,
shapes and textures.
They ask the spirits of rock and sky,
cholla and piñon, elk and coyote
to live awhile within them,
inhabit their creations.
The weavers sing songs of blessing and thanks
to the Creator who has shown them
sight as well as insight,
who has given them a glorious gift
for the translation of visions,
passed as yarn through fingertips.

In Vallecitos, New Mexico

We could've turned around
in that driveway in Vallecitos
where we stopped to check the map;
and I should have known
it was a bad plan
to keep going on that road
by the look on the faces
of those two ranchers unloading hay
as they watched us drive by,
due north on a road
they knew would disappear
beneath snow drifts up ahead
beside the frozen river, become
impassable beyond Cañon Plaza.
We should've turned around then,
when I saw the laugh in their eyes,
there for a minute, but dimmed
when they turned back to work
and another day in poor Vallecitos
surrounded them again.

Labyrinth

La luna llena de Febrero,
the full moon of February,
shines down on mesas named Kitchen
Huerfano and Matrimonial,
walks its circular journey around the Earth,
changing its path each night,
but always returning to its beginning.

I walk below in this generous light
through a labyrinth of stone and sand,
my path turning in unexpected places
as I spiral away from the moon's glow,
then feel its light again on my face.
I watch where my feet fall
lest I lose the path,
though I walk this maze
in hope of losing myself—
my ego, even my name for a while,
searching for the moment
I no longer notice my shadow dance,
even in this silvery light.

That Damn Apple

While walking a trail through the desert
a trinity appears to me,
dressed in the guise of three burros
looking for a handout, perhaps a couple apples;
but all I can offer is to scratch their ears,
having eaten my apple long ago
in the mist and myth of history,
hungry, at the time,
for the knowledge of evil and good.

The sky is infinite and blue
as the Virgin of Guadalupe's gown;
noon-length shadows dance around
cholla cacti and desert piñon
as I work with calloused hands
by the cursed sweat of my brow,
to earn another meal of daily bread
before the moon rises over the mesas,
wishing I'd never eaten that damn apple.

IV. *Inside a Greater Light*

Waterfall

The Cross River,
sliding over bedrock,
shatters into a galaxy of liquid crystals,
each filling itself with its own light,
singing its own song;
then bursts again
into a billion more singing lights
and then a billion more
before rejoining the flow
through time and space.
I watch this river fall three days
before I begin to understand.
Each of us must sing our own song
while seeking harmony;
must carry our own light
inside a greater light.
We cannot be still.
This is not the time for silence,
darkness.

Eleven Whitetail Deer

appear at dusk as if out of air.
I see them
only when they paw the snow
for winter-dry swamp grass
in the very place I was looking
just a minute ago
and saw nothing but bare tamaracks.

After the crescent moon rises
and the deer know my dog is in for the night,
they wander into the yard, one at a time,
feed on corn and sunflower seeds,
soft apples thrown under the bird feeders.

All I have is all I have now—
a herd of whitetail deer where there were none.
They vanish again, like days,
when I turn my head,
close my eyes for just a moment.

Crab Apple Trees

I'm tempted to say these trees belong to me,
take credit for blossoms that gather sunrise
like stained glass windows,
because eighteen springs ago
I dug holes for a couple scrawny seedlings,
spread their roots in a bed of manure,
watered them, supported them with stakes and twine
until the saplings could stand alone in the wind.
But now, the flowering crabs in my yard,
like grown children, have business of their own,
bumblebees to feed,
and small sour balloons to inflate
by the time autumnal flocks
of robins and cedar waxwings
come to them for sustenance.
My reward is in the way my eyes
gorge on brilliant blossoms,
the sweet aroma my nose inhales
like a rich dessert
in a restaurant for the senses.

The Chestnut Mare

The chestnut mare
grazing in my neighbor's pasture
is not my horse,
but she comes running when I whistle,
black tail and mane flying,
hooves drumming the earth,
knowing I carry apples in my pocket.
My face reflected
in the lake of her soft brown eyes,
proof of existence,
is all I dare ask of life.
I hold an apple in my open hand,
an offering to a gentle goddess,
entreating her not to blink.

Tree Planting Poem

Shovel in hand, I split the sod,
invade the country of bones,
spread a delicate filigree of roots,
give this seedling
to the care of earth and sky
and gods I cannot see.
I ask welcome for roots and branches,
then ask for acceptance of my watery cells
when I return for my own planting,
that I may rest a while
before sprouting again
in whatever form earth offers to sun.

birches

birches undress
like a woman
drops a golden gown,
stand naked,
fallen foliage
at their feet
the way a candle
stands smoldering
in a pool
of its melted self.

Prairie

Being a lover of horizons,
I love you
Without tearing your topsoil.
I harbor no desire for fences
Nor row crops to bind your seasons
Of black-eyed susans and periwinkle
Like sheaves of captive wheat.
I seek only to be the sunset
Resting on your earthy bosom.

Black-eyed Susans

Black-eyed Susans
set roots
amid purple prairie stars
on this glacial gravel ridge,
poke yellow heads
above little bluestem.
Black eyes look to the sky
like a farmer,
not asking for much;
for water and sun
in just the right amount,
at just the right moment;
not asking for much;
asking for everything.

Frost

Cassiopeia drapes her sparkling robe
over fireweed and goldenrod.
Trellised vines hang limp
as discarded snake skins
and marigold blossoms, brown and brittle,
rattle like husks of love, abandoned.
The stored fires of maple trees
are eaten by their roots
the way a sleeping bear
lives off its own fat over winter,
the way lovers grown old
live off the fat of youthful passion.

A Minor Death in Indigo

A single indigo bunting,
blue as the Virgin's gown,
flits up and down
between a bare branch of sumac
and sunflower seeds spilled on the ground.
Like a trout fly, skillfully tied,
played in the current by an expert fisherman,
it lures me out of my body,
into the sky.
I forget myself for just a moment,
forget even to breathe,
then gasp for breath;
a minor death in indigo,
then, rebirth.

Peat Fire

Years of accumulated rage or fear or sorrow
you thought safely buried, converted to fertile soil,
can smolder underground for years,
burn like a peat fire thought extinguished,
dressed in flowering dogwood and jewelweed,
undetectable behind eyes calm as summer sky.
Then suddenly a smoke wraith appears,
a small flame licks a stand of dry cattails,
a twig, a half-rotted log,
and soon the whole swamp erupts.
All the beautiful animals inside you panic;
frogs seek moist mud to bury themselves
in vain during this drought,
turtles cook inside their shells,
thrush and vireo nests turn to ash,
eggs fry in the heat.
You pray for a three-day soaker
before the fire spreads
to the houses of those who live near you.
You bring in all the fire suppression you can muster,
helicopter drops of clenched fists and teeth,
ceaseless pacing and praying;
you try to douse the fire with drink
though you know alcohol is fuel for fire;
you set backfires with cigarettes and weed,
and after awhile the fire seems extinguished,
but the old folks will tell you
the fire has only retreated below ground again
where hot spots can smolder even under a blanket of snow.

Coyote

Coyote prowls the swamp behind my house,
searching for a duck or goose nest
hidden in tall yellow grass,
thinking of eggs for breakfast,
perhaps a downy duckling or gosling,
maybe some baby mice for dessert.
Coyote sniffs around the nests people make, too;
people who seem unaware,
can't sense coyote's presence anymore,
so go about their business
as if coyotes are merely the stuff of old stories.
They seem surprised when coyote finds their nests,
say things like "We didn't have a clue."
or "It came right out of nowhere."
or "It happened so fast."—
poor excuses for inattention, sleep-walking,
made after coyote has ravaged their nests,
scattered sticks and moss and grass,
then laughs about it when the moon is full.

And There Are Coyotes

that prowl the land inside you, too,
seeking to feed on fears
you thought hidden even from yourself
like prairie dogs in their dens.
Damn those coyotes, so wily,
digging up burrows,
feeding on carcasses;
they survive all the poisons
you douse your insides with,
the traps you set,
laugh at bounties on their hides.

Cousin Coyote

Cousin Coyote is calling,
crooning a moon-mist tune,
a song that raises my hackles,
perks up my floppy ears,
brings a whine
from deep in my throat.

Though I'm bound to this house,
dependent on these people—
a bond I cannot break;
I listen to coyote's howl,
dream of prowling wood and bog
untethered.

While the humans sleep,
I hold coyote's song inside,
though unsure what it means.
My canine heart beats faster
as I give ear to cousin coyote
singing his old song of moonrise.

Domesticated

My old yellow dog hears them first—
coyote pups, yipping in the tamaracks,
trying out new voices,
singing ancient songs
in the hollow of night.
I wake when the dog perks up,
his stifled whine
humming into a sharp bark
as the coyotes yipping song echoes
through the overturned world
of tamarack roots lacing the darkness.
Hearing this eerie coyote chorus
makes the hair on my neck stand up;
the dog's hair bristles.
He looks at me, then back to the window
as if to say "Listen,
we both need to hear this."

This Hanging On

As deer flies buzz around my head,
my first thought is to catch a couple
for the featherless little phoebe, eyes not yet open,
fallen from its nest beneath our house's high eave,
miraculously landing in a flower pot.
Trying to keep it alive, we fed it flies,
poking them deep into its gaping beak
the way its mother would.
But the tiny bird died as we slept last night.
A day later, out of habit or forgetfulness
I still try to snatch flies out of mid air,
though I've already buried the little bird
out behind the wood pile.
It's just the way we were meant to be,
this hanging on to each other,
this clinging to any little life that's touched ours.

Fish in a Ditch

Some son of a bitch,
threw some fish in a ditch;
that's a fact,
they were stacked like cordwood,
wasted lives left to rot in the sun,
though they'd become a bountiful feast
for ants and flies and other agents of decay,
maybe a meal for a prowling coyote
or feral cat, cadaver-cleaning crows, certainly.
But given the news of the world,
heard on the same day
I biked by the discarded fish—
stories of hungry people,
decimated by typhoons, earthquakes, and politics,
I knew I had a poem to write,
present the facts, at least, since it was too late
to feed anyone this squandered protein;
if nothing else, let everyone know,
as if a poem could change anything,
that some son of a bitch
threw perfectly good fish in a ditch.

Crow on the Left Field Fence

A lone crow
perches on the left field fence,
heckles every batter,
cackles and squawks at every call
the umpire makes,
hops from one foot to the other
as he raucously caws at the left fielder
every time a ball is hit his way.
He doesn't really care
about baseball at all,
he's just passing time
on a Sunday afternoon;
he ain't root, root, rootin'
for either team,
just wants the ol' ball game
to end, the park to empty,
so he can fly under the bleachers,
look for peanuts and crackerjack,
maybe some shiny pop tops
to deck out his dugout.
If pickin's are slim
he may never come back.

Great Grey Owl

The footprints I've left behind me
in twilight-blue snow
have followed me down deer trails
criss-crossing in this silent bog
where I chance upon a dead owl,
a great grey owl, its feathery cowl
frozen solid in ice at the base
of a naked tamarack tree,
its bones gnawed by mice it once hunted,
its flesh reincarnated;
its owly call now a coyote's howl
or a crow's raucous yell
singing a song of death become life
that wakes someone up
like a poem crying to be written.

Elephant Bell #2

I've gone and done it,
struck this thick brass bell
with its padded mallet,
sent its deep bass song
into the ether.

A reckless act, I know,
having read that elephants
can hear each other call
from miles and miles away
and no doubt can hear
the song of this bell as well.

I think, what have I done?
It may take them awhile,
but I know there are elephants,
trunks swaying,
ears flapping,
tails wagging,
shaking the earth with each step,
surely on their way,
and I wonder what I'm going to do
when the elephants arrive.

V. *Arrogant Bones*

Arrogant Bones

A broke-down old farm house
sinks into South Dakota prairie;
the ground here, not fussy,
will eventually eat everything
placed on its plate
that the wind doesn't take first,
including families foolish enough to think
they could make a living with a bunch of kids
and that old steel-wheeled McCormack
rusting away out back;
but the soil's going to eat that, too,
along with the stones tilting over arrogant bones
that thought their houses of flesh
would never succumb to fatal prairie gravity.

Redwood County

Three piles of rubble—
one, the old farmhouse, itself,
pushed over by a front-end loader;
another, the bulldozed out buildings, the barn;
the last pile, broken branches and shorn roots
of the windbreak north and west of the farmstead,
no longer breaking the dirty wind
howling from all the way across South Dakota
or maybe Mongolia.

When I come by here again in November
the rubble has been burned,
ashes hauled to a landfill.
There won't be a sign next spring
in the freshly-plowed soybean field
of a family's story that took place
when there was new paint on a prairie farm house,
when the barn was full of hay and didn't sag,
when driven snow settled down in a little grove.

Barn

Rusty nails
with nothing to do in old age
but soak up sun,
protrude from the weathered oak ribs
of a sway-backed old barn,
think how it would be
to be silver and useful again,
holding tight a new wooden skin
that keeps at bay the wind
whistling through this rattling skeleton,
how it would be
for the barn to be filled up again,
warm beef in its belly,
dry hay in its head.

That's Me, That's You

They think, I'm joking,
these young women I work with,
when I point at this old man
walking past the La Playette,
the town walker, all ruffled and dirty,
and I say, that's me.
But they wouldn't think it so funny
if I pointed at the old women,
mostly widows, leaning on each other
as they leave church every morning,
and say that's you.

Old Crow

Somebody keeps the old man pretty clean.
His shirt hangs out of his baggy pants,
buttoned straight most days.
His boots are new; he needs good boots,
walking all over St. Joseph, talking to himself,
collecting aluminum cans and squawking too loud
about nothing that makes any sense
to the customers at the bait shop or hardware store.

I wonder if the old crow nests with his own children
or someone else's nestlings,
paid monthly with a government check
to keep him warm and fed and give him a room
with a TV and a window from which he can watch
his stash of aluminum cans, bagged in plastic,
glistening in moonlight.

I'd like to retrace the old crow's migrations
back thirty, thirty-five years,
just to see if his tracks in the snow resemble mine.
I'm curious about what I'll be collecting,
whose feathers I'll ruffle when I unravel,
my eyes turn yellow and I can't pass by shiny things.

Territory

I

The old dog's territory is shrinking.
He can barely walk up the hill to the mailbox with me,
But he goes out a of duty and loyalty only dogs possess.
On our return, he pauses at the bottom of the porch steps,
Seemingly psyching himself for the climb.
He spends the day lying on the deck, nose in the breeze,
Depends on the wind to inform him of goings on
In the woods and fields he used to roam,
Watches rabbits he once would've scattered
With a growl, a leap and a chase.
He watches deer, brazen enough to eat from the bird feeders
And squirrels hold no interest whatsoever.

II

An old man shuffling down the walk to his mailbox
Thinks about using a cane, but fears the cane will be followed
By a walker, then, my god, a wheelchair.
He looks to the blue sky at the end of the street,
The horizon that once called to him, but now seems a prison wall.
He's still got his memory, but even that is sporadic, undependable;
Bringing uncalled images he would rather forget as often as not.
The old man's not ready to lie down just yet,
So he shuffles along the best he can, unsteady though he may be,
Feels his territory shrinking—an apartment, a room, a bed,
Eventually a small pine box, a small hole in a big earth.
He hopes for a heaven so wide, he'll never find the end of it.

Ghost Towns

Victim of tornado, the economy,
a railway abandoned, a highway rerouted
or just all the young folks moving on,
looking for something better;
any sun-baked little town
could end up dead and gone
as a cool breeze trying to sneak
across Kansas in August.
You won't find
Kill Creek, Colorado
or Lonetree, North Dakota
or Boggy Depot, Oklahoma
on a map anymore,
much less on the ground;
they've melted away like a pat of butter
out on the hot pancake plains;
disappeared into the prairie,
not even a lick of syrup left;
time and wind, bad luck or chance
having scoured the plate of any evidence
that anything at all had ever been here,
much less that these places ever fed anyone,
body or soul.

Barely Believable

A chamomile breeze
riffles blue-eyed grass,
black-eyed susans, lulled
beneath eye-squinting sun,
the same way time passes—
hardly perceptible,
barely believable.
Faded daydreams lie tangled
in the roots of little bluestem
waving over unmarked graves
in forgotten cemeteries
beneath an endless sky.
Like the wind,
where do we begin,
where do we end?
Yet we trust in wind
to carry our names,
maybe speak them once in a while.

Picking Stones

Earth pulls everything into itself,
yet stones rise,
stones rise,
defying gravity it seems,
pulled into daylight
by seasons of freezing and thaw,
by the plows of sinking farmers.

The aching backs of field workers,
loading stones onto wagons,
see neither irony or mystery in this,
watching the sun sinking into the horizon,
bringing blessed love, drink or sleep,
knowing the sun will rise again tomorrow,
bringing more stones out of the earth with it.

Preparing the Fields

Before the land could be seeded
in barley, wheat and corn,
the prairie had to be plowed under;
swishing, swaying bluestem burned.

Before the land could be pastured
with cattle, horses and sheep,
there were bison, bear and wolves to kill,
singing swamps to drain and fill.

Before the land could be resettled,
there were thirty-eight black-eyed Sioux,
chanting aloud, heads unbowed,
to hang by their necks in Mankato.

At the Trampled by Turtles Concert

During intermission
at the Trampled by Turtles concert
a pretty blond girl, a stranger
forty years younger than me,
stops me and slurringly says
TxT fucking rocks!
And I say, no shit, they rock!
She gives me a high five and a hug
that dissolves our difference in age.
I return to my seat,
heart dancing in my chest
like the bass players fingers
dancing across guitar strings and frets,
blessing whatever gods
who brought about this brief encounter,
this random connection, bridging time;
but cursing the gods who must be laughing
at the joke they're playing on me,
unaware that I'm laughing, too,
and the joke's really on them.

The Gap Between

Driving through Kit Carson, Colorado
on the way to community service in New Mexico,
the young people with me in a crowded van,
plugged into ipod ear buds,
have no notion, or worse, no curiosity
about who Kit Carson was,
no clue about Chivington as we pass through there,
no idea of what happened at nearby Sand Creek.
I'm judging them, perhaps unfairly, I know,
but they are judging me, too,
because I've never watched the Simpsons
and don't get what happened to Homer
in the episode when he...
and how that relates to anything.
In the darkness outside Bent's Fort,
driving the speed limit through the present,
I'm wide awake between the past and the future,
while everyone else in the van sleeps
the sleep of those being taken for a ride.

Searching for a Curandera

I've looked in the yellow pages,
the want ads in the local dailies and weeklies,
bulletin boards in the feed mill,
hardware store, grocery store, drug store,
even the burrito joint in St. Cloud.
I can't find a curandera, not one,
not in Stearns County, Minnesota.

I'm left with a technological cure,
appointments in the medical mall,
doctors with stethoscopes around their necks,
laptops on their laps,
exam rooms small as bathrooms, sterile and bland,
science up the ying-yang (mine),
not to mention insurance forms, release forms,
next of kin forms.

What I want is an fat old woman or a skinny old man
with the moon shining behind their eyes:
a hut with a swept dirt floor,
a black kettle boiling over an open fire,
sweet smoke fanned at me with a peacock feather,
incantations, crushed herbs, rattles and drums.
I want to pay with a chicken
or tomatoes from my garden.
I want to be cured without getting sicker.
I want to live long and prosper.

VI. *Between Mars and Mexico*

Mars

I keep my distance, a low orbit;
send probes—
eyes, ears in your direction,
bounce subtle signals off your surface,
hoping for a sign, seeking clues
to what lies beneath the skin
of the planet that is you.
I see promise hidden
beneath what you choose to reveal
but a landing seems fraught
with danger, uncertainty.
I could burn up or crash
and I fear you'd not even notice,
you seem so distant, at times,
though I swear I've seen you blush,
even wink at me in the dark.

Coal Train

The only trains that rumble through here anymore
are these long-ass coal trains, rockin' and rollin',
haulin' what used to be Montana prairie,
stripped away and dug up after a couple million years
of doin' just fine, thanks.
Couple hundred cars, day after day after day,
clickin' and clackin' through every crossing
between Montana coal fields and Minnesota power plants,
whistle screamin' "Get the hell out of my way,
don't you know people in Minneapolis are afraid of the
dark?"

Darjeeling

A small, gracious brown-skinned man,
hands rough, yet delicate,
hands me a cup of steaming Darjeeling.
The tea picker smiles, bows, backs away.
I accept the cup
as if the tea is owed to me,
as if the man is my servant;
likewise I arrogantly accept this poem
rising in steam.
My own eyes, reflected in the tea,
look back at me as I drink.
I can't avoid them.
They tell me everything
is reflection.

Entering Yankton, South Dakota

The sun
rises from a bed of orange peel
while the moon
settles into a lavender blanket
covering the sleeping plains.
The Missouri River,
below this odd two-level bridge,
carries these ancient lights,
through a land that has painted itself
dried brown and gold, gray-skied.
My eyes gather all this;
my spirit seems flooded
with grace uncontained as the prairie.

You Give Me an African Sunset
(for Adrienne Stohr)

I imagine the setting sun
painting the west sides of Kitwe's houses with fire
as it slides down into the forest,
its heat lingering in the darkness around you
as you watch, thoughts of your Alaska home
noisy in your head as jungle insects.
In a letter, you dedicate this sunset to me.

I give you the first snow of this Minnesota winter.
I'll catch snowflakes on my tongue for you
and when the ground is covered
I'll roll in the snow until my clothes are soaked
and my skin tingles and reddens.
I'll make a thousand snowballs for you
and try to throw them all the way to Zambia.
If you catch one
you can carry it around on your head until it melts,
drips down over your face and neck and shoulders
runs under your shirt and into your pants.
You can do an African snow dance
for Bamayo and Bitatu and all the rest of your family
as they clap and smile and sing a song of you,
you crazy red-haired one, who makes them laugh.
You give me an African sunset,
I give you a blizzard.

Tourist Attraction

On Madeline Island, in the archipelago
of the yellow-breasted woodpecker,
Anishinaabe bones
lie in the "be sure to see" Indian cemetery,
a tourist attraction on a spit of bedrock,
thinly covered with soil,
just deep enough for graves,
between the Great Lake and a marina
sheltering sailboats and yachts
whose sailors live in land-locked Minneapolis.

Birthplace of the Anishinaabe people,
these islands, called the Apostles now,
are a place for tourists.
Each day, some stand silently, read faded headstones;
perhaps feel as I do, a trespasser, out of place.
Mainlanders leave the cemetery,
stroll past the marina, thoughts distracted
by huge white sails, billowing like avarice,
mahogany decks smooth and shiny as jealousy;
perhaps feeling a poverty of spirit.
Though crashing waves erode our shores,
we should be mindful
that faded names on broken stones
anchor our existence.

Wind Cave

Be wary of the human heart,
be it your own or that of another;
no one knows what lies beyond
the next curve in the tunnel,
carved by running blood.
Be wary of this heart,
laced with narrow passages,
dead-end hallways, unknown rooms;
surfaces that can cut with just a touch,
places blacker than any night
that ever darkened a day.
Be wary of the human heart.
There are those
who have never found their way out,
confused by all the drumming.

Jewel Cave

There are more crystal caverns,
worm holes and unexplored rooms,
more dead-end tunnels
beneath these tectonic wrinkles
than will be found in many lifetimes,
said the guide, leading us into the earth.
Amen to that, I concurred,
thinking of my human soul,
the little I've discovered in my short time;
how much wonder and how much darkness
lies beyond the flickering candle
I've been given to carry through this dark maze.

Dumpster Diving in the Garden of Eden

Six lovely red, unspoiled apples
lay atop a heap of typical American trash,
call me with a snake-like hiss,
feast on us, feast on us, feast on us.
Come on, Adam; it's why we exist.
But you're in a dumpster, I reply,
mingled with garbage, waste, refuse.
What about germs, sanitation, hygiene?
What about my middle-class American pride?

Alongside the apples, a stained newspaper
speaks headlines of disaster—
starving children in Myanmar, Dharfur,
the refugee camps in Syria and Uganda.
I think the sin, not that original in this land of plenty,
would be to let these apples rot, so I pluck them
from the trash, take them home, devour them,
their sweet juice running down my throat
as I write a check to a local food shelf
to assuage the guilt only the full-bellied feel.

Mexico

Gringos from el norte
visit for a week in winter
(two if you're the boss)
in search of sun
and the bottom of another margarita,
while in Juarez, piscadoras,
workers with sore backs
and squinting eyes
bend over benches
in bad light,
place chips in computer boards
all day every day
for nothing but a few tamales
so the gringos
can have the whole enchilada
shipped back up north
real cheap.

VIII. *I Should've Taken Creative Writing*

Welding Class

The minute I walked into that welding class
I knew I didn't belong.
The other guys, all younger than me,
seemed to know each other and the instructor, too.
I could tell by the way they sparked their torches,
how they adjusted the oxygen and acetylene
to make a flame of just the right combination
of orange and blue fire
while I fumbled with the igniter and knobs on my torch,
producing only a stench of unburned gas,
that I should've taken Creative Writing 1 instead.

I stuck it out a couple classes,
even managed to lay down a few good beads,
though most were too far apart or piled on each other
like a heap of dead turtles.
It took a while, but I finally discovered words
can burn like hot slag falling on your boot,
or cut anything better than a hot flame,
can hold things together as strongly as a good weld.

Border Crossing

Trying to enter the Pentameter of Iambia
In the land of Academia,
My car is inspected at the border
By metric poetry guards, uniformed sonnets
Wearing epaulets of rhyme scheme insignias.
I have nothing to declare, I declare.
No shit, they smugly say
After finding free verses hidden
In the trunk, taped to the wheel wells,
Bolted behind the bumpers, sewn in seat cushions.
I'm rudely turned away,
Told to throw away my notebook, find a textbook.
Don't come back until I meet their criteria.
As I drive away I give them the finger
In my rear-view mirror,
Grateful, I guess, I didn't have to confess
My paranoia of poetic inferioria.
My secret is safe with Victoria.
My poems still play in Peoria.

Check-up Poem #2

When the doctor asked me what I do,
I wanted to say I'm a poet,
but I was afraid the doctor would say
No, really, what do you do,
for a living, I mean?
And unless I lied, I'd have to say,
Well, poems are what makes me live.
But the doctor would probably say,
No, no. What pays the bills?
(meaning the doctor bill, especially)
and so I told the doctor I'm a recycler,
I sort other people's garbage.
The doctor seemed to think that was all right
and she asked me if I had any lower back pain.
I said, "No, not if I do my stretches everyday,
but she never asked me about the pain of poetry
and how that hurts, especially when I stretch.

Dirty Hands

Grease and machine oil
fill every crack in my fingers
and the palms of my hands.
At break time and lunch time
I scrub my hands
with a stiff-bristle brush
and pink hand cleaner from the dispenser
hanging above the slop sink,
make my hands clean enough
to eat a doughnut and a sandwich
but not clean enough for making love.

At home, I scrub them again
with pumice soap and a scouring pad.
Even after a hot-water soaking
my hands, white and wrinkled, appear clean
but after they dry I still see ground-in grease
and I think my hands will never be clean
any more than the words in my head
will ever be cleaned into poetry,
no matter how many times
I drag them across a new page,
hoping to wear away the accumulated grit
of words that attach themselves to feeling,
but serve only to hide what can't be said.

Don't Listen to Leonard Cohen

Don't listen to Leonard Cohen
if you're trying to write a poem.
You can't measure up to Leonard,
the language, the images, the meter;
you'll just end in gasping frustration,
burning your notebook,
breaking your pencils,
maybe slitting your wrists,
though the image of blood on a blank page
might possess a certain Cohen-ness
if paired with accordions and cellos, pianos,
a guitar with tears falling on its strings,
burning violins.

There are no oranges from China in your life,
no gypsies dance around a fire,
read palms in a moon-lit window;
the birds have all flown from the wire,
the midnight choirs are all shuttered
in this land of passionless bedrooms in dark farm houses,
asleep as deep as Lutherans with clear consciences
who would never sing with gravelly voices
of combing a woman's raven hair, anyway.
No, it would be best to remain asleep
in front of your TV, accept your ineptness;
you'll just end up writing hokey lines like
Don't listen to Leonard Cohen
if you're trying to write a poem.

About the Author

Larry Schug has worked as a dish washer, grave digger, bookstore clerk, groundskeeper, junk yard laborer, assembly-line worker, forestry technician, fire-fighter, and farm worker. He is currently employed as Recycling Coordinator at the College of St. Benedict in St. Joseph, Minnesota, where he has been employed for thirty-one years.

Larry is the author of four books of poems—*Scales Out of Balance* (1990), *Caution: Thin Ice* (1993), *The Turning of Wheels* (2001), all published with North Star Press of St. Cloud, Inc., and a chapbook, *Obsessed with Mud*, published by Poetry Harbor, Duluth, Minnesota. *Caution: Thin Ice* was a 1993 Minnesota Book Award nominee. Schug has won two Central Minnesota Arts Board grants, a 2007 Pushcart Prize nomination and was awarded a 2008 McKnight Fellowship for Writers. He has also received recognition for poems in *The Talking Stick* and *Prairie Poetry*.

Larry lives beside a large tamarack bog with his wife, Juliann Rule, dog, Mojo, and cats, Darwin and Wendel, in St. Wendel Township, Minnesota.